The
RECOVERY
ROSARY

"Those in recovery are a testimony to the truth that the Rosary has an evangelical character, and I am very grateful to the brave men and women who are willing to share with us how Christ has changed their lives. My prayer is that these meditations assist in bringing the mysteries of the Rosary to life not only for people struggling with various addictions but for all members of the Church, because we are all in need of encountering Jesus in a concrete and incarnational way."

Fr. Sean Kilcawley, STL
Pastor of Sts. Leo and Martin Parish
Palmyra, Nebraska

Catholic in Recovery Participants

"*The Recovery Rosary* is a beautifully-crafted resource for those struggling with their own or a loved one's addiction. It is both profound and practical—a guiding light for anyone on the path to healing."

James T.
Arizona

"This book is a spiritual sanctuary for those affected by unhealthy attachments. *The Recovery Rosary* beautifully integrates meditative prayer with recovery principles, providing a compassionate and effective guide for healing. It's a gift of hope for families and individuals alike."

Sarah R.
Missouri

"This book transforms the Rosary into a powerful ally in the battle against addiction. Its practical support and spiritual nourishment make recovery not just a goal but a deeply enriching journey. Highly recommended for anyone seeking true healing."

Ellen D.
New Jersey

The
RECOVERY ROSARY

Meditations for Those Impacted by Addiction, Compulsions, and Unhealthy Attachments

 Catholic in Recovery

Compiled and Edited by Scott Weeman

Ave Maria Press AVE Notre Dame, Indiana

Scripture texts in this work are taken from the *New American Bible, revised edition* © 2010, 1991, 1986, 1970 Confraternity of Christian Doctrine, Washington, DC, and are used by permission of the copyright owner. All Rights Reserved. No part of the New American Bible may be reproduced in any form without permission in writing from the copyright owner.

Nihil Obstat: Reverend Monsignor Michael Heintz, PhD
Censor Librorum
Imprimatur: Most Reverend Kevin C. Rhoades
Bishop of Fort Wayne–South Bend
Given at Fort Wayne, Indiana, on January 16, 2025

© 2025 by Catholic in Recovery

All rights reserved. No part of this book may be used or reproduced in any manner whatsoever, except in the case of reprints in the context of reviews, without written permission from Ave Maria Press®, Inc., P.O. Box 428, Notre Dame, IN 46556, 1-800-282-1865.

Founded in 1865, Ave Maria Press is a ministry of the United States Province of Holy Cross.

www.avemariapress.com

Paperback: ISBN-13 978-1-64680-391-0

E-book: ISBN-13 978-1-64680-392-7

Cover image © Sebastian Gollnow/picture alliance via Getty Images.

Cover and text design by Andy Wagoner.

Printed and bound in the United States of America.

Library of Congress Cataloging-in-Publication Data is available.

CONTENTS

Introduction **vii**

What Is Catholic in Recovery? **xi**

How to Pray the Rosary **xiii**

The Joyful Mysteries **1**

The Luminous Mysteries **27**

The Sorrowful Mysteries **53**

The Glorious Mysteries **77**

Additional Prayers **103**

INTRODUCTION

The Recovery Rosary: Meditations for Those Impacted by Addiction, Compulsions, and Unhealthy Attachments offers recovery-focused meditations for all twenty mysteries of the Rosary: the Joyful, Luminous, Sorrowful, and Glorious Mysteries. Each meditation features a relevant excerpt from scripture or a papal document, a personalized reflection written by a member of the Catholic in Recovery (CIR) community, and three questions to prompt deeper meditation and intimacy with Jesus and Mary—all through a perspective of addiction recovery. You may want to keep a journal of your responses to the reflection questions that accompany each mystery of the Rosary.

The twenty meditations you are invited to pray with in this book come from deep within addiction and recovery experiences, including alcoholism, drug addiction, lust-related addictions, compulsive eating behaviors, and loved ones of an addict. Each mystery is considered in light of the Catholic tradition as well as the Twelve Steps of recovery, offering hope, wisdom, and encouragement to all those seeking to overcome addictions, compulsions, or unhealthy attachments as well as their loved ones. Meditations include reflection questions on both the Bible passages that begin each mystery and the written reflections to help prompt individual contemplation as well as group discussion. Those impacted by the family spiritual disease of addiction will find value in reframing "your addictions, compulsions, or unhealthy attachments" to "your experience with family addiction" when considering these reflection questions. The reflections themselves also serve as testimonials, indicating how others have found freedom and healing through the Twelve Steps and their relationship with Jesus and Mary.

How to Use This Meditation Book

This reflection book is an aid to maintaining conscious contact with God through reciting and meditating on all twenty mysteries of the Rosary. The Rosary is a beautiful form of meditative prayer steeped in Catholic history and tradition, one that has been practiced by countless faithful Catholics for several hundred years (see page xiii to learn how to pray the Rosary). The Rosary invites us to meditate on the mysteries of Christ's life, death, and resurrection while repeating some of the Church's most ancient and beloved prayers, such as the Our Father, Hail Mary, and Glory Be. It offers us a method of prayer to help us grow closer to Christ through the prayerful and tender intercession of our Blessed Mother.

The *Catechism of the Catholic Church* explains:

> "The Church's devotion to the Blessed Virgin is intrinsic to Christian worship." The Church rightly honors "the Blessed Virgin with special devotion. From the most ancient times the Blessed Virgin has been honored with the title of 'Mother of God,' to whose protection the faithful fly in all their dangers and needs." . . . The liturgical feasts dedicated

Introduction

to the Mother of God and Marian prayer, such as the rosary, an "epitome of the whole Gospel," express this devotion to the Virgin Mary. (971)

This reflection book is intended to be a spiritual touchstone as you meditate on the Rosary, bringing to life each mystery and its meaning as it relates to people in recovery and those who love them. You might refer to this book during your own personal prayer time, exploring the questions provided at the conclusion of each mystery while lifting your heart to God and/or journaling your responses. If you participate in a Catholic in Recovery meeting or some other faith-based group (whether explicitly recovery related or not), your group may use the reflections to help foster a space for deeper spiritual sharing in light of the insights, testimonials, and wisdom shared in these reflections. Since the meditations are written to provide a certain measure of depth and insight, completing a set of five mysteries in one sitting will likely take forty-five minutes to an hour. Allow for a deep and profound experience of this beautiful Catholic prayer practice.

We pray that *The Recovery Rosary: Meditations for Those Impacted by Addiction, Compulsions, and Unhealthy Attachments* can be of value to you along your recovery and faith journey.

WHAT IS CATHOLIC IN RECOVERY?

Catholic in Recovery (CIR) is a community that provides hope and healing to individuals and families impacted by addictions, compulsions, and unhealthy attachments by integrating 12-step recovery principles with the sacraments and traditions of the Catholic Church, ultimately bringing souls to Jesus Christ.

CIR accomplishes this mission by:

- uniting community members through recovery meetings rooted in 12-step recovery principles, sacred scripture, and traditions of the Catholic Church in alignment with her magisterium;

- hosting retreats and events where attendees grow closer to God and each other through the sacraments, shared testimonies, workshops, and fellowship;

- providing resources that guide individuals toward a spiritual awakening and encounter with Jesus Christ through the Twelve Steps and the sacraments;

- encouraging members to form a supportive relationship with both a sponsor and a home group; and

- educating and forming clergy, seminarians, and community leaders on how to support individuals and families impacted by addiction.

Catholic in Recovery began in 2015 to unite individuals and families seeking freedom from the darkness of addictions, compulsions, and unhealthy attachments, including alcoholism, drug addiction, compulsive eating behaviors, lust/sex addiction, gambling addiction, codependency, technology addiction, cluttering, emotional challenges, grief, and fear. The first CIR group started meeting in San Diego in 2017, launching a fellowship that, at the time of printing, is active in nearly 140 parishes throughout North America and reaches around five thousand people weekly across the world via virtual meetings.

HOW TO PRAY THE ROSARY

Texts for the prayers of the Rosary follow these instructions.

1. Make the Sign of the Cross.
2. Holding the crucifix, pray the Apostles' Creed.
3. On the first bead, pray an Our Father.
4. Pray one Hail Mary on each of the next three beads.
5. Pray the Glory Be.
6. For each of the five decades, announce the mystery (perhaps followed by a brief reading from scripture such as those found in this book); then pray the Our Father.
7. While fingering each of the ten beads of the decade, say one Hail Mary and meditate on the mystery. After praying the ten Hail Marys, pray the Glory Be. After finishing each decade, some say the Oh My Jesus prayer requested by the Blessed Virgin Mary at Fatima, which you can find on page xvi.
8. After praying the five decades, pray the Hail, Holy Queen, followed by this dialogue prayer:

V. Pray for us, O holy Mother of God.

R. That we may be made worthy of the promises of Christ.

Let us pray: O God, whose Only Begotten Son, by his life, Death, and Resurrection, has purchased for us the rewards of eternal life, grant, we beseech thee, that while meditating on these mysteries of the most holy Rosary of the Blessed Virgin Mary, we may imitate what they contain and obtain what they promise, through the same Christ our Lord. Amen. ("How to Pray the Rosary," USCCB, https://www.usccb.org/how-to-pray-the-rosary)

Prayers of the Rosary

Apostles' Creed

I believe in God,
the Father almighty,
Creator of heaven and earth,
and in Jesus Christ, his only Son, our Lord,
who was conceived by the Holy Spirit,
born of the Virgin Mary,
suffered under Pontius Pilate,
was crucified, died and was buried;
he descended into hell;
on the third day he rose again from the dead;
he ascended into heaven,
and is seated at the right hand of God the Father almighty;
from there he will come to judge the living and the dead.

I believe in the Holy Spirit,
the holy catholic Church,
the communion of saints,
the forgiveness of sins,
the resurrection of the body,
and life everlasting.
Amen.

Our Father

Our Father, who art in heaven,
hallowed be thy name;
thy kingdom come;
thy will be done on earth as it is in heaven.
Give us this day our daily bread;
and forgive us our trespasses
as we forgive those who trespass against us;
and lead us not into temptation,
but deliver us from evil.
Amen.

Hail Mary

Hail Mary, full of grace, the Lord is with thee;
blessed are you among women, and blessed is the fruit of
    thy womb, Jesus.
Holy Mary, Mother of God, pray for us sinners,
now and at the hour of our death.
Amen.

Glory Be

Glory Be to the Father, and to the Son, and to the Holy Spirit;
as it was in the beginning, is now, and ever shall be, world without end.
Amen.

Oh My Jesus

O my Jesus, forgive us our sins, save us from the fire of hell,
lead all souls to heaven, especially those who are in most need of thy mercy.
Amen.

Hail, Holy Queen

Hail, Holy Queen, Mother of Mercy,
our life, our sweetness, and our hope.
To thee do we cry,
poor banished children of Eve;
to thee do we send up our sighs,
mourning and weeping in this valley of tears.
Turn, then, most gracious advocate,
thine eyes of mercy toward us,
and after this, our exile,
show unto us the blessed fruit of thy womb, Jesus.
O clement, O loving,
O sweet Virgin Mary.
Amen.

THE JOYFUL MYSTERIES

The First Joyful Mystery

THE ANNUNCIATION

Hear the Word of God
In a group setting, one person reads aloud. For individual use, read silently:

> In the sixth month, the angel Gabriel was sent from God to a town of Galilee called Nazareth, to a virgin betrothed to a man named Joseph, of the house of David, and the virgin's name was Mary. And coming to her, he said, "Hail, favored one! The Lord is with you." But she was greatly troubled at what was said and pondered what sort of greeting this might be. Then the angel said to her, "Do not be afraid, Mary, for you have found favor with God. Behold, you will conceive in your womb and bear a son, and you shall name him Jesus. He will be great and will be called Son of the Most High, and the Lord God will give him the throne of David his father, and he will rule over the house of Jacob forever, and of his kingdom there will be no end. . . . The holy Spirit will come upon you, and the power of the Most High will overshadow you.

The Joyful Mysteries

Therefore the child to be born will be called holy, the Son of God." . . . Mary said, "Behold, I am the handmaid of the Lord. May it be done to me according to your word." (Luke 1:26–38)

Share aloud in a group or read in silent reflection when praying alone.

- What words or images stand out to you in this reading?

- What feelings do these stir in you, or what do they cause you to think about?

- How do you want to respond to this mystery of the Annunciation?

Pray a Decade of the Rosary
(see page xiii for instructions if needed)

A Meditation from Stephanie N.

As I reflect on this mystery, it seems appropriate to begin the Joyful Mysteries with an example of humility, a virtue that is perfectly demonstrated by the Blessed Virgin Mary in the annunciation. The Catechism of the Catholic Church states that "humility is the foundation of prayer. Only when we humbly acknowledge that 'we do not know how to pray as we ought,' are we ready to receive freely the gift of prayer" (2559). She desires only the will of God, never counting the personal costs. Mary does this not only at the moment of the annunciation but also constantly throughout her life. This, however, is the preeminent event of her profound humility. I am also struck by how this mystery relates to recovery. It demonstrates the inseparability of Mary from her son, Jesus, who literally dwells within her womb. This truth parallels our call to let Jesus dwell within us as redeemed sinners seeking recovery from addictions, compulsions, and unhealthy attachments. Mary is our perfect model of how to live within the fullness of and in union with God's heart.

I recall when our Blessed Mother opened my heart in a way only a true mother could, so gently and personally. I was reading Luke's account of the annunciation and wondered what it must have been like for her to conceive while unmarried. I'm adopted, and while I have very little information about my biological parents, I do know that my birth mother was young, unmarried, and that she named me Mary. For the better part of my life, I couldn't reconcile that I could be "good fruit" since I was unplanned and conceived illegitimately. The Blessed Mother would eventually expose these as lies, but until then I lived out of defensiveness and shame. I acted out belief in these lies in the form of anorexia. I desired to hide and disappear, literally trying to hide and disappear my body.

The Joyful Mysteries 5

Growing up Catholic, I knew the story of the annunciation, but when I read Luke's account, it was like I was experiencing it for the first time. Mary was unwed at the time of the Incarnation, and yet there was no hint of shame—only of God's greatness and her desire to do his will. I perceived a gentle voice reminding me of Psalm 139: "For you created my inmost being; you knit me together in my mother's womb." Mary and her spouse, the Holy Spirit, guided me to the truth! It all seems so obvious now, but it was radical news at the time. God willed the Incarnation, and Mary cooperated, just as he had willed my being through my birth mother. But I was afraid of this insight and knew I would need a safe and faith-filled place to find healing. I knew Jesus was the answer and that I had an addiction to my unhealthy relationship to food. Soon I found Catholic in Recovery. Soon I found healing and home.

Let us contemplate God's greatness in this most sacred event, which offers us a type of paradox. While an "annunciation" is typically broadcast publicly to a wide audience, it occurs privately here to a single soul, Mary. God, who alone can do all things, is pleased to depend on this ordinary young woman to manifest his saving grace. In desiring only to do God's will, Mary is humble in her greatness and great in her humility—she is the perfect model for us. May we regularly look to Mary as our model of humility as we grow closer to Christ, her son, in our faith and recovery journeys.

Pray in silence for a few moments.

Make It Personal

Share in your group or reflect in silence or by journaling if praying alone.

- How does the mystery of the Annunciation speak to you personally about your addictions, compulsions, or unhealthy attachments as well as your recovery?

- How does or might Mary's "fiat" help you place more trust in God's plan for your life?

- Have you ever experienced an unmistakably personal message in prayer, and if so, how did you respond?

The Second Joyful Mystery

THE VISITATION

Hear the Word of God
In a group setting, one person reads aloud. For individual use, read silently:

> During those days Mary set out and traveled to the hill country in haste to a town of Judah, where she entered the house of Zechariah and greeted Elizabeth. When Elizabeth heard Mary's greeting, the infant leaped in her womb, and Elizabeth, filled with the Holy Spirit, cried out in a loud voice and said, "Most blessed are you among women, and blessed is the fruit of your womb. And how does this happen to me, that the mother of my Lord should come to me? For at the moment the sound of your greeting reached my ears, the infant in my womb leaped for joy. Blessed are you who believed that what was spoken to you by the Lord would be fulfilled." (Luke 1:39–45)

Share aloud in a group or read in silent reflection when praying alone.

- What words or images stand out to you in this reading?

- What feelings do these stir in you, or what do they cause you to think about?

- How do you want to respond to this mystery of the Visitation?

Pray a Decade of the Rosary
(see page xiii for instructions if needed)

A Meditation from Karen D.

Every time I pray the Rosary now and reach the mystery of the Visitation, I rejoice along with Elizabeth: "And how does this happen to me, that the mother of my Lord should come to me?" If I wrote about every moment I've experienced the mystery of her presence in recovery, it would fill an entire book! February 2, 2005, was the day when everything changed. God's pervasive grace was infused into a transformative moment of reckoning. Finally willing and desperate enough, I came back to AA, asked for help, and began working the Steps. Recovery became my only priority, and I finally believed for the first time that if I thoroughly followed the path, I would find freedom.

Like some of you, I came into recovery with grief and deep loss over my relationship with my mother. What I learned was that our addictions, compulsions, and unhealthy attachments are but symptoms of a deeper spiritual malady. My journey home to the fullness of our Catholic faith has been aided by Mary, her presence, her divine touch, and a love that only the mother of our Lord could give. Jesus sends his mother to the lost, the sick, and the suffering, as he did for me.

In April 2010, my family and I moved away from everything a good foundation of recovery provides, including my AA and Methodist church families. Feeling like I had been dropped off in the middle of a desert, three years later and eight years into my sobriety, I began longing to know everything about Jesus. Step 12 stayed at the top of my heart and mind, and I recalled that the surest pathway of healing is to be of service to those around us. Yet, where could I be of service to those in my midst?

By seeking, praying, and discerning (Step 11), a most remarkable encounter transpired, one that I will never forget and will always be etched into my heart. At 4:40 in the morning of December 19, 2013, I awakened to a voice—a lady's voice. It was an indescribable sound of purity, beauty, kindness, and clarity, a bright crispness that cannot be explained. The voice exclaimed, "Karen!" I immediately sat up, filled with expectancy, and felt God's presence in my heart and spirit.

At the time, there was a long-term care facility that I passed weekly only one mile from our neighborhood on the way to the grocery store, where I would see the direst of situations. Prompted by the Blessed Mother's loving voice—the gentle calling of my name—I decided to visit the long-term facility on Christmas Eve a few days later to sing Christmas hymns. I began going back every week to prepare a Bible study and get to know the residents there, listening to their stories and praying with them. I had my prayer answered in how to live out Step 12 and be of service to others. The residents became my friends, my blessings, and through obedience to God's urging, my healing. I found the pearl of great price, and the relationships I formed there eventually provided the steps that led to my coming into the Catholic Church.

Recovery teaches spiritual progress, not perfection, which is a profound yet simple truth. Just as Elizabeth recognized Mary's faith and trust that "what was spoken to [her] by the Lord would be fulfilled," we too can trust in God's promise of healing through our faith and recovery journey. God sent his mother to deepen my faith and love of Christ, and lead me into his sacramental Church. May all of us who have suffered or still suffer from addictions, compulsions, and unhealthy attachments allow Mary a visitation within our hearts. May we allow her faith and confidence in her son to inspire our own faith through service to others and rejoice always in her presence!

Pray in silence for a few moments.

The Joyful Mysteries   11

Make It Personal
Share in your group or reflect in silence or by journaling if praying alone.

- If Mary came to visit you, what would you want to say to her, and how would you respond?

- Is there a door in your heart that is closed, and if so, what steps could you take today to open it to Jesus and Mary's loving presence?

- How might Jesus and Mary be nurturing a call within your heart to serve others who have been wounded as part of living out Step 12?

The Third Joyful Mystery

THE NATIVITY

Hear the Word of God
In a group setting, one person reads aloud. For individual use, read silently:

> While they were there, the time came for her to have her child, and she gave birth to her firstborn son. She wrapped him in swaddling clothes and laid him in a manger, because there was no room for them in the inn. Now there were shepherds in that region living in the fields and keeping the night watch over their flock. The angel of the Lord appeared to them and the glory of the Lord shone around them, and they were struck with great fear. The angel said to them, "Do not be afraid; for behold, I proclaim to you good news of great joy that will be for all the people. For today in the city of David a savior has been born for you who is Messiah and Lord. And this will be a sign for you: you will find an infant wrapped in swaddling clothes and lying in a manger." (Luke 2:6–12)

Share aloud in a group or read in silent reflection when praying alone.

- What words or images stand out to you in this reading?

- What feelings do these stir in you, or what do they cause you to think about?

- How do you want to respond to this mystery of the Nativity?

Pray a Decade of the Rosary
(see page xiii for instructions if needed)

A Meditation from Kathy B.
Even though the Holy Family had meager surroundings that first Christmas, I can imagine how much joy they radiated. When I reflect on this mystery, I can't help but think about one particular Christmas I had as a child. I grew up in a large Catholic family of ten, and Christmastime was usually very hectic since my parents struggled to make ends meet. Placing high expectations on presents, decorations, and special church clothes always seemed to supersede the true meaning of the humble beginnings of Christ's entry into the world on that cold, dark night in a stable. Even still, one Christmas memory that I will always cherish is caroling with my family.

With a scribbled playlist in our pockets, we forged hand in hand down the snowy pathway, spying for well-lit houses, on a mission to spread our love and Christmas cheer to all who would listen. With each knock came a look of surprise and warm welcome from friends and strangers alike as we sang "Joy to the World," radiating the Holy Family's joy from that first Christmas. Oh, how I wish those joyful times remained as I grew from a child into adolescence! They didn't.

The innocence of my youth was stained when someone I loved molested me. My first thought was that it felt good, but knowing that it was wrong, I was ultimately left with constant anxiety, confusion, and inner turmoil. I didn't tell anyone and set out on a path of self-sabotage, grabbing at anything or anyone to help make the pain go away. My parents took us to church but never modeled any semblance of a healthy relationship with others, let alone God. They fought all the time, specifically over money. How did they cope with the stressors of life or the difficulties of parenthood? By drinking, smoking, gambling, cussing, and carousing. The holy sacrament of Confession was embraced not as a gift of God's healing grace but as a punishment for bad behavior, and I worried that "my secret" would send me to hell.

In high school, I met a boy who made me feel special. It wasn't long before we were using drugs and drinking together, followed quickly by unprotected sex. I became pregnant, and instead of responding with faith and trust in God, like Mary had, my immediate response was that of paralyzing fear and despair. I convinced myself the situation was hopeless. I succumbed to the lies of society and the gentle coercion of others and sacrificed my child, and another soon after, by having two abortions.

I spiraled out of control using alcohol, drugs, and sex to numb the deep pain, guilt, and shame for years. I recall many times where I felt the presence of God, but I stayed locked in the darkness where there was no hope of rescue. Then one day, God broke through the madness, and I declared aloud, "I need help!" I surrendered and became honest, open-minded, and willing to do anything. With the fellowships of AA and Catholic in Recovery, I was set on a course of action, one that required change and self-sacrifice. The Twelve Steps eventually led me to seek help from "Project Rachel" to heal from my abortions. I was given a second chance, and God conceived in me a new life of peace and healing. I was reborn!

And so it is for all of us who have struggled with addictions, compulsions, and unhealthy attachments—we are invited to be reborn in freedom and hope as we meditate on the birth of our Savior in this mystery. And when we surrender and are reborn in Christ's love, we are able to shine his light and proclaim with great love, "Joy to the world!"

Pray in silence for a few moments.

Make It Personal
Share in your group or reflect in silence or by journaling if praying alone.

- What gifts of recovery bring you great joy that you feel called to share with others?

- Are there wounds from your past blocking you from allowing God's peace to be born in your heart, and if so, how can you take steps today toward healing?

- How have you made room in your heart for the Christ child to rest by working the Twelve Steps of recovery and engaging in the sacramental life of the Church?

The Fourth Joyful Mystery

THE PRESENTATION

Hear the Word of God
In a group setting, one person reads aloud. For individual use, read silently:

> Now there was a man in Jerusalem whose name was Simeon. This man was righteous and devout, awaiting the consolation of Israel, and the holy Spirit was upon him. It had been revealed to him by the holy Spirit that he should not see death before he had seen the Messiah of the Lord. He came in the Spirit into the temple; and when the parents brought in the child Jesus to perform the custom of the law in regard to him, he took him into his arms and blessed God, saying: "Now, Master, you may let your servant go in peace, according to your word, for my eyes have seen your salvation, which you prepared in sight of all the peoples, a light for revelation to the Gentiles, and glory for your people Israel." (Luke 2:25–32)

Share aloud in a group or read in silent reflection when praying alone.

- What words or images stand out to you in this reading?

- What feelings do these stir in you, or what do they cause you to think about?

- How do you want to respond to this mystery of the Presentation?

Pray a Decade of the Rosary
(see page xiii for instructions if needed)

A Meditation from Kevin S.

The reflection calls to mind my own "presentation" to the Lord when my parents had me baptized as an infant. When I came to the age of reason and beyond, I had to make the conscious choice to present myself continually to the Lord of my own accord. Coming of age in the early seventies, I fell prey to many of the temptations particularly facing teenagers at the time, especially alcohol. However, I rekindled my faith during my senior year of high school, making my Confirmation and turning away from drinking. For several years, I practiced and grew in my faith.

My life ebbed and flowed, personally, professionally, and spiritually. Although still not a drinker at that time, a couple years after college, I joined the US Navy, and particularly in my warfare community, drinking was a mark of membership. I succumbed to the chameleon in me and joined the revelry. Had not my parents presented me for Baptism, though? Had I not been living a life of faith as a living sacrifice to the Lord? Yes, but as a Southern Baptist pastor once told me, "The problem with living sacrifices is that they tend to crawl off the altar." And crawl off the altar I did. At one point during my addiction to alcohol when I was still *mechanically* practicing my faith, in a small Bible study group we considered the well-known story of Abraham being asked to sacrifice Isaac, his beloved son, to God. The reflection question was, "What is your Isaac?" In other words, what is the dearest thing in your life that you need to offer to God? I responded with something about my profession, money, comforts, but inside I was screaming, "My consumption of alcohol!" I had a case of "self-will run riot." Alcohol was at that time my true higher power. It took a while for me to enter recovery, and I only did when I got sick and tired of being sick and tired.

As we enter recovery from our addictions, compulsions, and unhealthy attachments and present ourselves to God, we are born again into a new life of healing and sobriety. As critical as this first step is—our initial "yes" to recovery—we are encouraged to regularly present our whole being to God as we journey in recovery. The Big Book of *Alcoholics Anonymous* states, "What we really have is a daily reprieve contingent on the maintenance of our spiritual condition" (85). For us Catholics, that also means remaining in a state of grace with active participation in the sacraments, particularly the Sacraments of Reconciliation and the Eucharist, both of which reinforce our recovery and spiritual development.

Whether we came into recovery already Catholic or have entered the Church since embarking on our recovery journey, we are often called upon to publicly reaffirm our baptismal vows, our presentation to God, by renouncing Satan and all his works and surrendering ourselves to the triune God. While we do this from time to time during the liturgy of the Mass, we can also do this on our own to begin each day—as a way of maintaining conscious contact with the Lord. So, let us renew our baptismal vows today to help us in our recovery journey as we meditate on the mystery of the Presentation.

Pray in silence for a few moments.

Make It Personal

Share in your group or reflect in silence or by journaling if praying alone.

- How have you continued to "present" yourself to Father, Son, and Holy Spirit as you work your recovery?

- What aspects of your life have you not totally surrendered to the Lord?

- What people in your life are you being asked to "present" to God in trust, letting go of your attempt to control or manage them?

The Fifth Joyful Mystery

THE FINDING OF JESUS IN THE TEMPLE

Hear the Word of God
In a group setting, one person reads aloud. For individual use, read silently:

> Each year his parents went to Jerusalem for the feast of Passover, and when he was twelve years old, they went up according to festival custom. After they had completed its days, as they were returning, the boy Jesus remained behind in Jerusalem, but his parents did not know it. . . . After three days they found him in the temple, sitting in the midst of the teachers, listening to them and asking them questions, and all who heard him were astounded at his understanding and his answers. When his parents saw him, they were astonished, and his mother said to him, "Son, why have you done this to us? Your father and I have been looking for you with great anxiety." And he said to them, "Why were you looking for me? Did you not know that I must be in my Father's house?" But

The Joyful Mysteries 23

they did not understand what he said to them. (Luke 2:41–50)

Share aloud in a group or read in silent reflection when praying alone.

- What words or images stand out to you in this reading?

- What feelings do these stir in you, or what do they cause you to think about?

- How do you want to respond to this mystery of the Finding of Jesus in the Temple?

Pray a Decade of the Rosary
(see page xiii for instructions if needed)

A Meditation from Pete S.

I can only imagine Mary and Joseph's anguish at losing Jesus on their return journey home. The fear, panic, and uncertainty when they discovered the child Jesus was missing must have been agonizing. In all honesty, the depth of their helplessness was probably not too much unlike what my wife must have experienced the many times she found me after another episode of binge drinking, wondering if I was going to live or die. Or how my friends and family must have felt when I repeatedly scared and embarrassed them with my irrational behavior. Or how my children must have felt wondering why their dad was so emotionally unpredictable and so often neglectful of their need for love and attention.

Like Mary and Joseph, everyone who cared for me felt at times a sense of powerlessness when it came to not knowing what to do or how to reach me. And this sense of powerlessness was something I also experienced when, in those infrequent and brief moments of honest clarity, I knew my life had become deeply disordered and destructive. But the pain of that realization was so great that it would evoke an overwhelming sense of hopelessness, which I could not bear. This then drove me to act out again and again, plunging me ever more deeply into the enslaving cycle of addiction. I was a lot like the poet Dante when he wrote, "I found that I was in a gloomy wood, because the path which led aright was lost" (*Inferno*, canto 1). I truly had no idea how I got there or how to find my way out!

Our Lord responds to Mary and Joseph's desolation with the unexpected yet consoling words "Why were you looking for me? Did you not know that I must be in my Father's house?" In sharing the truth of who he was by stating where he was, Jesus was in effect delivering a subtle rebuke to their lack of trust and resultant anxiety by revealing that he was fulfilling the will of his father. And I think our Lord's words to Mary and Joseph are instructive for us in recovery because a significant reason why we become addicted in the first place is that deep down inside we fundamentally lack trust and live in a kind of

The Joyful Mysteries

perpetual and ruthless fear. We do not trust that our suffering has a purpose and so flee from pain by self-medicating in our temporary, illusory pleasures. We do not trust that we are loved or even lovable at all and so dissociate from God and others as a kind of self-protection in the fantasies of our addictions, compulsions, or unhealthy attachments. And worst of all, we often fall into the heresy that we cannot be forgiven, that our habitual addictive sins are just too great. We lose trust that God's mercy is truly infinite and inexhaustible.

All of these responses represent expressions of pride and self-will, the root cause of the spiritual disease of addiction. Our pride leads us to reject Christ's invitation to unite our suffering with his for the redemption of souls, which is the fullest expression of sacrificial love. We absurdly reject our belovedness as sons and daughters of God, the very culmination of God's creation and so precious to Jesus's Sacred Heart. And we assert our dominion over God by refusing to receive his mercy.

The remedy is humility and contrition of heart, what conversion in recovery teaches us. In a certain sense, Jesus's words to Mary and Joseph reveal his own more probing questions to each of us in recovery: Why were you looking for me in all the wrong places and things? Why did you hate yourself so much and believe you were beyond my mercy? Did you not know that I do not hate you? Do you not believe that I love you beyond your wildest imagination and that I forgive you out of the immeasurable depths of my love if you would only receive it?

Pray in silence for a few moments.

Make It Personal

Share in your group or reflect in silence or by journaling if praying alone.

- How did powerlessness play a role in fueling your addictions, compulsions, or unhealthy attachments?

- How have you come to embrace your powerlessness in recovery as the pathway to peace?

- How was the sin of pride the real culprit in the enslaving madness of your addictions, compulsions, or unhealthy attachments?

THE LUMINOUS MYSTERIES

The First Luminous Mystery

THE BAPTISM OF JESUS

Hear the Word of God
In a group setting, one person reads aloud. For individual use, read silently:

> Then Jesus came from Galilee to John at the Jordan to be baptized by him. John tried to prevent him, saying, "I need to be baptized by you, and yet you are coming to me?" Jesus said to him in reply, "Allow it now, for thus it is fitting for us to fulfill all righteousness." Then he allowed him. After Jesus was baptized, he came up from the water and behold, the heavens were opened [for him], and he saw the Spirit of God descending like a dove [and] coming upon him. And a voice came from the heavens, saying, "This is my beloved Son, with whom I am well pleased." (Matthew 3:13–17)

Share aloud in a group or read in silent reflection when praying alone.

- What words or images stand out to you in this reading?

- What feelings do these stir in you, or what do they cause you to think about?

- How do you want to respond to this mystery of the Baptism of Jesus?

Pray a Decade of the Rosary
(see page xiii for instructions if needed)

A Meditation from Jana I.

I can only imagine what Jesus must have experienced after he was baptized, the heavens were opened, and the Spirit of God descended upon him. It must have been a profound spiritual experience for Jesus. When I became sober on July 19, 2020, I too felt the Spirit of God descend upon me. This is not something that I can easily put into words. For me, it was a feeling of being connected to God. It was a feeling of knowing God is always with me—that I am not alone. It was a feeling of relief knowing that God is in control. To this day, there is still an entire committee of voices in my head, but now God is the head of that committee, so to speak. What a relief to know that God will comfort me, give me strength and peace if only I submit to him. I recognize now that I always had this gift of faith before me, but I had to choose it. God was always holding this gift out to me, waiting patiently for me to ask for and receive his Spirit, just like Jesus did in this mystery. Jesus models for us the perfect and constant acceptance of God's Spirit.

When I was in the midst of my addiction to alcoholism and life presented challenges, my fears would take over and I would get angry at God. My doubts, despair, and defeat made me turn my back on him. I turned to the darkness of my addiction rather than the light that only God can provide. I was hopeless, dying a spiritual death. And this spiritual death brought me to a crossroads where I ultimately had to choose the path of darkness or the path of light. I couldn't grasp surrendering to God's will until I was completely hopeless and had no choice but to rely on God—I had hit my rock bottom. I finally accepted the gift of my faith, asked God for help, and completely surrendered. Through this surrender, I was reborn into a new way of life.

Through both Baptism and recovery, we are all born into a new way of life. In this new life, we recognize our identity first and foremost as beloved children of God. We stop our self-seeking ways and become followers of Christ. We recognize that the Holy Spirit dwells within us, and our empty, dark, and hopeless souls suddenly gain light and hope. We gain new insight and learn to see things from God's perspective. By regularly surrendering to God's will, we receive the gift of sanctifying grace.

Personally, doing these things has been instrumental in keeping me sober. It is only by the grace of God that my desire to drink has been removed. I continue to receive this grace

The Luminous Mysteries

by turning my life and will over to the care of God, one day at a time. As the Big Book of *Alcoholics Anonymous* states, "We have found much of heaven, and we have been rocketed into a fourth dimension of existence of which we had not even dreamed." We can all experience this fourth dimension—this profound spiritual experience—when we surrender regularly to God and are born again to a beautiful life of hope, faith, and freedom.

Pray in silence for a few moments.

Make It Personal
Share in your group or reflect in silence or by journaling if praying alone.

- How has recognizing the gift of your Baptism played a role in your recovery?

- Have you experienced glimpses of the "fourth dimension," and if so, what have these been like for you?

- What do you do regularly to remain open to God's help and grace in your life?

The Second Luminous Mystery

THE WEDDING FEAST AT CANA

Hear the Word of God
In a group setting, one person reads aloud. For individual use, read silently:

> On the third day there was a wedding in Cana in Galilee, and the mother of Jesus was there. Jesus and his disciples were also invited to the wedding. When the wine ran short, the mother of Jesus said to him, "They have no wine." [And] Jesus said to her, "Woman, how does your concern affect me? My hour has not yet come." His mother said to the servers, "Do whatever he tells you." Now there were six stone water jars there for Jewish ceremonial washings, each holding twenty to thirty gallons. Jesus told them, "Fill the jars with water." So they filled them to the brim. Then he told them, "Draw some out now and take it to the headwaiter." So they took it. And when the headwaiter tasted the water that had become wine. . . . Jesus did this as the beginning of his signs in Cana in Galilee

and so revealed his glory, and his disciples began to believe in him. (John 2:1–11)

Share aloud in a group or read in silent reflection when praying alone.

- What words or images stand out to you in this reading?

- What feelings do these stir in you, or what do they cause you to think about?

- How do you want to respond to this mystery of the Wedding Feast at Cana?

Pray a Decade of the Rosary
(see page xiii for instructions if needed)

A Meditation from Jeff R.

"Do whatever he tells you." I'm struck by just how simple this phrase is as I reflect on this mystery. So simple, yet so powerful. It sums up how we are called to live as Christians—as followers of Christ. Our Blessed Mother doesn't have a lot of dialogue in the gospels, but what she says here speaks volumes. I'm also struck by the fact that Jesus performs his first miracle at a wedding feast. In the gospels, Jesus compares

The Luminous Mysteries 35

his relationship to us, his Church, as one of a bridegroom to a bride. The sacrament of the marital bond is therefore very important to him, and he wants to have a similar relationship with each of us. And this relationship involves love. Not a romantic love but an unconditional love—the type of love the Father has for us.

Through the worst of my alcoholism and other unhealthy attachments, my wife stuck by me and helped me through thick and thin. She embodied the vow of "for better or for worse," though there were a lot of "for worse" moments. Yet, it was her unconditional love—a love like God's love for us—that helped me make it to where I am today. That love made me appreciate God's unconditional love for me. My wife also kept me grounded, encouraging me to always look to the Lord for guidance in the midst of my suffering. She was my Mary, in a sense, reminding me to "do whatever he tells you."

Of course, love is necessary not only for marital relationships but also for all our relationships. Addictions, compulsions, and unhealthy attachments can strain or destroy the love shared in our relationships with our spouses, children, family members, and friends. I was blessed to have a family who was supportive of my journey of recovery, and I may not have stayed on the path of recovery if it wasn't for their help. This is why Steps 8, 9, and 10 are so important—they remind us of the importance of making amends with others for the wrong we've done and maintaining healthy relationships with all those in our lives. By working to rekindle and heal those bonds with our loved ones, we find increasing support through their love to grow in our recovery and faith. Mary's words, "Do whatever he tells you," remind us also to keep our Lord's commandments, which overlap with working the Twelve Steps as we seek to get in harmony with ourselves, our loved ones, and God. Mary, as our loving mother, keeps us focused on the *right* things. She keeps us focused on God, by pointing to her son, who is the way, the truth, and the life.

Pray in silence for a few moments.

Make It Personal
Share in your group or reflect in silence or by journaling if praying alone.

- Who is (or was) like Mary to you, the one who keeps you on track and points you toward the Lord on your recovery journey?

- How does your personal relationship with God resemble a marital relationship?

- How has your recovery benefited from the unconditional love of others?

The Third Luminous Mystery

THE PROCLAMATION OF THE KINGDOM

Hear the Word of God
In a group setting, one person reads aloud. For individual use, read silently:

> After John had been arrested, Jesus came to Galilee proclaiming the gospel of God: "This is the time of fulfillment. The kingdom of God is at hand. Repent, and believe in the gospel." (Mark 1:14–15)

Share aloud in a group or read in silent reflection when praying alone.

- What words or images stand out to you in this reading?

- What feelings do these stir in you, or what do they cause you to think about?

- How do you want to respond to this mystery of the Proclamation of the Kingdom?

Pray a Decade of the Rosary
(see page xiii for instructions if needed)

A Meditation from Marty T.

As I reflect on the mystery of the Proclamation of the Kingdom, I'm reminded of how I came to embrace the kingdom of God after years of alienation and pain. I spent the first twenty-six years of my life living in sin as an unbaptized heathen. I was a slave to alcohol, drugs, and sexual perversion. My life was so entangled in sin that at various moments I wanted to die and even attempted suicide. I was surrounded by nefarious people and almost joined the satanic church when I was twenty-one. I can look back now and see how God saved me from that decision. Unfortunately, it wasn't enough to get me to surrender my sinful life that was driven and fueled by my addictions, compulsions, and unhealthy attachments.

On November 12, 2000, I dropped to my hands and knees and begged God for help, yelling, "Why won't you let me die! I can't live like this anymore! Please help me! I will do anything!" That was the moment I surrendered and began to seek help, to seek the truth, to seek the kingdom of God. Shortly after that I was taken to a local psychiatric ward and treatment center, where I hopelessly thought I would spend my life locked away. However, God had another plan for me. A week after being in the psychiatric ward, I was offered help at a twenty-eight-day treatment center, where I was introduced to 12-step recovery. I met someone in the rooms of recovery who invited me to Mass one day, and for the first time in my life I felt a sense of home and belonging.

Soon after that, during the Easter Vigil, I was baptized and confirmed and received Communion for the first time. I felt and sensed a presence I had never known before. It felt like there was a vast host of angelic beings there that night at that church, which was also filled with hundreds of people. I truly believe that there were angels and saints there celebrating what God had done for me and the other candidates being received into the Church. I had experienced the kingdom of God on earth in a powerful way. Heaven and earth came together that night, and I was freed from the sins, addictions, compulsions, and unhealthy attachments that had nearly killed me.

The Twelve Steps, the sacraments, and the truths of our Catholic faith, as taught in Catholic in Recovery meetings, represent the Gospel that Jesus emphatically encourages us to embrace in this mystery of the Rosary. The Twelve Steps show us how to live the Gospel and reconcile with God, ourselves, and the people in our lives. As a result of faith and recovery, we are able to proclaim the same truth that Jesus proclaimed two thousand years ago to those who are just as hopeless and tired as I was over twenty years ago. We have the great privilege of being able to encourage and help others surrender their addictions, compulsions, and unhealthy attachments to God—to repent and believe in the Gospel—as a response to the kingdom of God being at hand. We get to show others how to believe and embrace the Proclamation of the Kingdom in union with the One who said, "I am the way and the truth and the life. No one comes to the Father except through me" (John 14:6).

Pray in silence for a few moments.

Make It Personal
Share in your group or reflect in silence or by journaling if praying alone.

- What actions can you take or have you taken to surrender and repent of your sins, addictions, compulsions, or unhealthy attachments?

- How have you or how can you experience the love and mercy of God through discovering his kingdom and its power to set you free from your addictions, compulsions, unhealthy attachments, or the family spiritual disease of addiction?

- What blocks you from totally giving yourself to the Gospel and allowing God to make his kingdom present in your heart?

The Fourth Luminous Mystery

THE TRANSFIGURATION

Hear the Word of God
In a group setting, one person reads aloud. For individual use, read silently:

> [Jesus] took Peter, John, and James and went up the mountain to pray. While he was praying his face changed in appearance and his clothing became dazzling white. And behold, two men were conversing with him, Moses and Elijah, who appeared in glory and spoke of his exodus that he was going to accomplish in Jerusalem. . . . Peter said to Jesus, "Master, it is good that we are here; let us make three tents, one for you, one for Moses, and one for Elijah." But he did not know what he was saying. While he was still speaking, a cloud came and cast a shadow over them, and they became frightened when they entered the cloud. Then from the cloud came a voice that said, "This is my chosen Son; listen to him." (Luke 9:28–35)

Share aloud in a group or read in silent reflection when praying alone.

- What words or images stand out to you in this reading?

- What feelings do these stir in you, or what do they cause you to think about?

- How do you want to respond to this mystery of the Transfiguration?

Pray a Decade of the Rosary
(see page xiii for instructions if needed)

A Meditation from Fr. Charlie B.

The Transfiguration reminds me of what are called *mystical experiences*, sometimes called *signal graces* or graces that *give signs*. An example is smelling roses while at prayer when no roses are present, seeing the sun glow or "dance" in the sky, or perhaps even sensing the presence of a dead loved one. People sometimes say, "I don't need a sign to believe in God." My response to that is, "How do you know what you need?" If the apostles needed this miraculous experience of the Transfiguration to prepare them for the upcoming atrocities of the Crucifixion, then who knows what we need to prepare us for future events in our lives?

The Luminous Mysteries

I was prepared to receive the grace of awareness that I was an alcoholic through the preparation of Alateen, a group that helps teens deal with alcohol-related issues, and being a junior counselor at eighteen years old in an alcohol treatment unit. Those experiences—those graces—helped me eventually recognize my own addiction and, through another moment of grace, admit my powerlessness over alcohol at twenty-six years old. Praise God! I truly believe it was a graced moment. And the same has occurred in my life with respect to quitting smoking cigarettes and other unhealthy inclinations.

Grace is defined as the very "life of God," and boy do we surely need a lot of it to get unstuck from the never-ending cycle of addictions, compulsions, and unhealthy attachments. God give us graces not only to overcome evil, sin, and weakness but also to fortify and ready ourselves for the plan he wants to accomplish through each of us, no matter how great or small. Beginning with the renewal of our lives with Steps 4 to 9, his plan for all of us is to give away the joy and freedom we've experienced in recovery through Steps 10, 11, and 12! Yet, we can only do this by surrendering to his will and responding freely to his many graces, even when we don't necessarily understand them.

Jesus tells us, "I came so that they might have life and have it more abundantly" (John 10:10). Sometimes this "abundance of life" comes in the form of something I may not have expected or even cared for at first, but again, what do I know? If his plan for me at times is to be overwhelmed or even unsettled by his grace—much like the apostles in this mystery—in preparation for what he has in store for me, then who am I to judge? We are called instead to accept his graces as they come, trusting that God knows what we can handle. With his help and by surrendering to him, we become part of his great plan of salvation and healing. That's faith. Help us, Lord, to do your will today and every day!

Pray in silence for a few moments.

Make It Personal
Share in your group or reflect in silence or by journaling if praying alone.

- Have you had any spiritual or mystical experiences in your life, and if so, how did you respond to them?

- How has the very life of God—his grace—influenced your faith and recovery?

- How do you show gratitude to God for all he has done for you?

The Fifth Luminous Mystery

THE INSTITUTION OF THE EUCHARIST

Hear the Word of God
In a group setting, one person reads aloud. For individual use, read silently:

> While they were eating, Jesus took bread, said the blessing, broke it, and giving it to his disciples said, "Take and eat; this is my body." Then he took a cup, gave thanks, and gave it to them, saying, "Drink from it, all of you, for this is my blood of the covenant, which will be shed on behalf of many for the forgiveness of sins. I tell you, from now on I shall not drink this fruit of the vine until the day when I drink it with you new in the kingdom of my Father." Then, after singing a hymn, they went out to the Mount of Olives. (Matthew 26:26–30)

Share aloud in a group or read in silent reflection when praying alone.

- What words or images stand out to you in this reading?

- What feelings do these stir in you, or what do they cause you to think about?

- How do you want to respond to this mystery of the Institution of the Eucharist?

Pray a Decade of the Rosary
(see page xiii for instructions if needed)

A Meditation from Ann A.

I learned an important insight by working the Twelve Steps of recovery—God does not expect me to be perfect. It's an insight I'm also reminded of as I consider this mystery and Jesus's institution of the Eucharist, which is an invitation to participate in God's love and life with my whole self, including my imperfections. I did not always understand this, and it took me a long time in recovery to become aware that I have been driven mercilessly by the false god of perfectionism. As a young girl, when my heart was open and vulnerable to being known, accepted, and loved, I internalized the belief that there was something

The Luminous Mysteries 49

wrong with me—that I was not good enough. My parents were affected by the family disease of alcoholism, passed down through generations. This sad legacy left me believing I was fundamentally flawed, unlovable, and unworthy. So, I set about trying to create a sense of worth on my own, thinking, *If I'm perfect, I might finally get others' approval, acceptance, and love.*

Of course, this was a recipe for failure. Perfection wasn't possible. There was no way to attain the standards I set for myself, and every failed attempt resulted only in my self-loathing. Every unmet expectation revealed I was not good enough. I berated myself, feeling intense guilt and shame. This perfectionism was destroying my life and relationships, especially my most important relationship with God. I believed that, although God loved me like my earthly parents, he was constantly checking boxes to keep track of how I was measuring up. I felt he must be perpetually disappointed by my failures. I believed I should be doing better before I came to him, but that moment never seemed to occur.

The good news is that we do not have to be perfect to encounter and experience God's love. The Eucharist is the most perfect example of God's free gift of love. There is nothing more precious in all of creation, and there is no possible way we can ever be "perfect" or "worthy" enough to earn it. There is nothing we can ever do to merit it. Yet, Jesus freely offers us his body and blood—his very life. When we celebrate the Eucharist, we can say "I am not worthy" without shame or despair. We can echo the great truth we learn in Step 1 of recovery—perfection lies only in our willingness to surrender to God's healing and grace. Ultimately, as we journey toward God through recovery and faith, it becomes not about our worthiness but about our willingness. It is about becoming childlike again so that we can be vulnerable and open to receiving God's love. By doing this, we are truly seen by God. We are known fully, accepted completely, and loved unconditionally. We are restored to our true selves as the children of God. And we come to accept that we are finally and completely worthy because he has made us so.

Pray in silence for a few moments.

Make It Personal
Share in your group or reflect in silence or by journaling if praying alone.

- How do the Twelve Steps help you to become childlike and vulnerable when receiving the Eucharist?

- How has your experience with addictions, compulsions, or unhealthy attachments affected your sense of self-worth?

- As one who was truly perfect and yet remained humble before God, how might the Blessed Mother be a model for your own approach to the Father?

THE SORROWFUL MYSTERIES

The First Sorrowful Mystery

THE AGONY IN THE GARDEN

Hear the Word of God
In a group setting, one person reads aloud. For individual use, read silently:

> Then they came to a place named Gethsemane, and he said to his disciples, "Sit here while I pray." He took with him Peter, James, and John, and began to be troubled and distressed. Then he said to them, "My soul is sorrowful even to death. Remain here and keep watch." He advanced a little and fell to the ground and prayed that if it were possible the hour might pass by him; he said, "Abba, Father, all things are possible to you. Take this cup away from me, but not what I will but what you will." (Mark 14:32–36)

Share aloud in a group or read in silent reflection when praying alone.

- What words or images stand out to you in this reading?

- What feelings do these stir in you, or what do they cause you to think about?

- How do you want to respond to this mystery of the Agony in the Garden?

Pray a Decade of the Rosary
(see page xiii for instructions if needed)

A Meditation from Sr. Margaret

This scene of Jesus on the eve of his most painful death is likely familiar to those of us who have struggled with addictions, compulsions, or unhealthy attachments as a way to avoid pain. We too have likely begged God to spare us from suffering—often suffering resulting from the consequences of our poor decisions and unhealthy behaviors. As I enter into these Sorrowful Mysteries in Jesus's life, I'm reminded to find new and healthier ways to pass through such painful moments. I ask myself, What is Jesus experiencing in the garden, and what does he do? How does he manage his own terrible suffering?

He immediately asks his friends to stay with him and watch with him as he nears the upcoming storm of his crucifixion. It's a good reminder of our need for fellowship. Then in their presence, Jesus begins to let go and *feel* that grief and distress. The *Revised Standard Version* of the Bible reads that "he threw himself onto the ground"! Surely, this will remind us of our own breaking point that brought us to the realization that we could no longer go on as usual, avoiding pain and difficulties by using food, alcohol, or other unhealthy substances and behaviors to distract ourselves from reality. Oh, how well I remember such a breaking point in my own life! For a few moments the possibility of taking my own life to end my pain crossed my mind. Thank God that his love and sanity took firm hold of me. Prayer became possible for me, and God—a "Power greater than myself"—could help. I surrendered to a loving God through a power beyond my own capacity.

As we reflect on Jesus's Agony in the Garden, we see the solution to dealing with any and all suffering. In his "deep distress," Jesus turns to his loving Father and honestly asks for what he wants, which is to not drink from this cup. But more deeply still, he then surrenders to his loving Father's will. He knows that God the Father is our Father, too, and that he will balance Jesus's request with our need for salvation. But that's not the end of it. Three times Jesus comes to his friends for support, only to find them asleep. Was he disappointed, hurt by their failure to stay awake and seeming indifference to his pain? In his selfless love, he focuses on Peter's needs instead of his own, telling him to pray that he does not come to his own trial. Jesus's instruction is an example for all of us to pray for God's help no matter what painful event we're experiencing and to accept that we don't suffer alone. And this reminder about how to respond to the reality of our brokenness keeps

The Sorrowful Mysteries 57

us reaching a hand out for Jesus who has walked the path of suffering before us. I'm so grateful that my weakness never puts him off. I never found him asleep when I have the willingness to ask for his help and presence!

And what's the outcome of Jesus's prayer in the garden? We witness his calmness and clarity of mission, saying, "Let us go. The time has come." This is the calmness and clarity that comes to us, too, when we have truly surrendered—given ourselves over to an acceptance that leads to action. When I have accepted my weaknesses and need for help and turned to God instead of food, I find God's will is good. Often painful, but always good. And he sends me signs, little miracles to let me know he is the rock on whom I can depend. We are safe when we surrender. We are safe when we continue to surrender and walk resolutely with him down the path leading through addiction and death to freedom and life.

Pray in silence for a few moments.

Make It Personal
Share in your group or reflect in silence or by journaling if praying alone.

- How is Jesus's response to his own suffering instructive for your struggle to surrender and maintain serenity in the face of trials?

- As Jesus faces his crucifixion, what feelings of his have you identified with in your own suffering?

- How have you struggled to accept God's will instead of your own?

The Second Sorrowful Mystery

THE SCOURGING AT THE PILLAR

Hear the Word of God
In a group setting, one person reads aloud. For individual use, read silently:

> Then Pilate took Jesus and had him scourged. (John 19:1)

Share aloud in a group or read in silent reflection when praying alone.

- What words or images stand out to you in this reading?

- What feelings do these stir in you, or what do they cause you to think about?

- How do you want to respond to this mystery of the Scourging at the Pillar?

Pray a Decade of the Rosary
(see page xiii for instructions if needed)

A Meditation from Juan Carlos P.

This mystery reminds me of a specific event in my own life. Among the many times I gave in to drinking and using drugs, one particular incident marked me deeply. I was kidnapped by corrupt policemen working for the Mexican cartel in Mexico. While seeking drugs in a very dangerous area, I was stopped by these men, beaten severely, and taken to an undisclosed location where I was held captive. The beating I received was indescribable, and at one point they decided to take my life. They drove me to a remote location, forced me to kneel, and pointed a gun at the back of my head. They pulled the trigger three times, but the gun never fired. They left me there, and hours later I was found.

As I reflect on Jesus taking that terrible scourging, I recall the whipping he bore for me. I believe Jesus took those bullets for me from that gun that didn't fire, saving me in that moment—just like the whipping he endured at the pillar. Yet, at the same time, I saw myself as the one whipping him, looking at him with a raging face as if I had never known him and hated him. This was an incredibly heartbreaking realization.

When I was a little boy, I always loved and believed in Jesus Christ. I knew he was there by my side. I could hear him, see him, and sometimes, when I closed my eyes, I felt transported into the stories of the gospels. This was similar to what I felt with the gun to my head, except I was seeing how my transgressions were now killing him. My addictions were like demons moving my hands to whip him, and yet, despite all that, he still took on suffering out of love for me. You would think that after this realization I would have stopped drinking and using, but sadly, things only got much worse—that's how lost I was to the insanity that is addiction. It would still be some time before I came to the rooms of recovery, driven by the gift of desperation. My life was falling apart, and I had lost the will to live. Reflecting on how Jesus was scourged at the pillar, I see how Jesus suffered for all of us struggling with addictions, compulsions, and unhealthy attachments. Despite being completely undeserving, he bore tremendous pain to save us from death and condemnation.

Having found sobriety and a solution in my 12-step recovery program and with Catholic in Recovery, I like to think that we have been given the opportunity to clean the wounds we inflicted and continue to inflict on Jesus. By turning our will and lives over to him and truly surrendering, we are granted the chance to be like Christ and take "bullets" for others. We do this when we don't react as we used to, keep our mouths shut and avoid seeking revenge, show compassion to those who have hurt us, and empathize with the pain others are experiencing. This Sorrowful Mystery helps us reflect on our transgressions against Jesus and find the grace to repent and change our ways as we contemplate the suffering that he endured for us. It also gives us the grace to see how he can transform our old, unhealthy behaviors into loving, kind, and selfless actions. As we practice our program of recovery, find solutions, and pass them on to those who still suffer, we can model, by God's grace, how Jesus turns to good what was originally meant for evil.

Pray in silence for a few moments.

Make It Personal
Share in your group or reflect in silence or by journaling if praying alone.

- Have you ever felt abandoned or left to die (physically, spiritually, or emotionally) only to realize Jesus was with you all along, and if so, what was that experience like?

- How have you experienced Jesus bearing scourgings and "taking bullets" for you in your recovery and faith journey?

- How can you be Christlike by bearing the sufferings of others as you accompany them in their recovery and 12-step journey?

The Third Sorrowful Mystery

THE CROWNING WITH THORNS

Hear the Word of God
In a group setting, one person reads aloud. For individual use, read silently:

> And the soldiers wove a crown out of thorns and placed it on his head, and clothed him in a purple cloak, and they came to him and said, "Hail, King of the Jews!" And they struck him repeatedly. Once more Pilate went out and said to them, "Look, I am bringing him out to you, so that you may know that I find no guilt in him." So Jesus came out, wearing the crown of thorns and the purple cloak. And he said to them, "Behold, the man!" (John 19:2–5)

Share aloud in a group or read in silent reflection when praying alone.

- What words or images stand out to you in this reading?

- What feelings do these stir in you, or what do they cause you to think about?

- How do you want to respond to this mystery of the Crowning with Thorns?

Pray a Decade of the Rosary
(see page xiii for instructions if needed)

A Meditation from Mark L.

Jesus is subjected to a vicious and sadistic assault by the Roman soldiers who beat him and affix a crude crown of thorns to his head. This physical torture is coupled with a psychological attack designed to humiliate and dehumanize him through mockery, derision, and contempt. The purpose of this particular torture is to render him worthless in his own eyes and in the eyes of others. After verbally tormenting him in his "crown" and "royal" purple robe, the soldiers' attempt to humiliate Jesus is broadened and made public when Pilate presents Jesus to the crowd in this dehumanized condition.

The private and public humiliation Jesus experiences in this mystery is something that speaks to my own experience of addictions. This is true for all of us struggling with addictions, compulsions, and unhealthy attachments. Deep shame, humiliation, and dehumanization result when we abandon our true identities as beloved children of God and give ourselves over to our vices. In the depths of my active sexual addiction, I engaged in anonymous sexual encounters with strangers, putting myself in physical and psychological danger in order to pursue a disturbed and distorted sexuality that had its roots in early childhood sexual abuse. The self-inflicted shame and sense of degradation that came after these encounters fueled a seemingly endless cycle of repetition that drained me of my humanity. I was powerless to stop the self-inflicted humiliation and abuse, and although my behavior never became public knowledge, the sense of degradation and humiliation was yet another secret that I carried with me each day. I was sure that no one could ever love me if they knew about the things I was doing as I lived a double life.

As we contemplate this mystery, it becomes clear that what Jesus offers us is a way out of humiliation, dehumanization, and despair. In his humility, Jesus suffers the humiliation and degradation on our behalf and shows us that we can choose to follow him and find respite and comfort. He has gone before us and knows what it is to be subjected to humiliation, degradation, and the pain of being dehumanized by shame, mockery, scorn, and contempt. While the life of active addiction perpetuates a misery that is only fully understood by Jesus and our fellow addicts, life in recovery presents a way to healing and wholeness if we are willing to surrender and follow him. In my active addiction, the dozens of anonymous encounters and countless hours spent in their pursuit left me exhausted and utterly hopeless. On many occasions, I wanted to abandon a particular pursuit but felt I had no right to change my mind and walk away if I had initiated that encounter. I reluctantly followed through with interactions that, paradoxically, had no addictive appeal simply because I believed I deserved anything that came as a result of my distorted pursuits. That type of surrender—the addictive antithesis of the surrender of recovery—did great damage to my emotional and spiritual condition. It made me believe that I was deserving of any and all horrific consequences. I believed that I was not worthy of living, and I was convinced that if I died, I would be damned.

As we encounter Jesus in scripture and our Rosary prayers and meditations, we see that he is making all things new (see Isaiah 43:19). Jesus transforms our humiliation into humility and shows us the strength that is found in relying on him to guide us. The depths of shame, degradation, and despair that typified our lives as active addicts are gradually diminished as we pursue the work of the Twelve Steps. Paired with our Catholic faith practices—the Mass, the sacraments, and our daily prayer life—the Twelve Steps lead us out of the darkness of addiction and its accompanying shame and degradation into the light of Christ in the renewal of recovery.

We must always remember that the word *recovery* means we are retrieving something we once had that was lost but never completely destroyed. We are now, and have always been, the beloved sons and daughters of a loving father who sent his son to save us from ourselves. It is this triumphant Christ who leads us from the darkness of addiction into the light of recovery. The crown of thorns intended as a gesture of mockery and humiliation has been transformed into a crown of victory for Christ the King!

Pray in silence for a few moments.

Make It Personal
Share in your group or reflect in silence or by journaling if praying alone.

- How have you experienced humiliation in your active addiction, compulsion, or unhealthy attachment?

- What are some of the barriers that keep you from viewing yourself as a beloved child of God, and how does this affect your recovery life?

- How does doing service work in your recovery program help you find purpose and embrace your identity as a child of God?

The Fourth Sorrowful Mystery

THE CARRYING OF THE CROSS

Hear the Word of God
In a group setting, one person reads aloud. For individual use, read silently:

> So they took Jesus, and carrying the cross himself he went out to what is called the Place of the Skull, in Hebrew, Golgotha. (John 19:16–17)

Share aloud in a group or read in silent reflection when praying alone.

- What words or images stand out to you in this reading?

- What feelings do these stir in you, or what do they cause you to think about?

- How do you want to respond to this mystery of the Carrying of the Cross?

Pray a Decade of the Rosary
(see page xiii for instructions if needed)

A Meditation from Talitha R.

The Carrying of the Cross has been a Sorrowful Mystery I've reflected on not only when praying my beloved Rosary but also as an alcoholic. Before recovery, I received each day as if I was living out this very gospel verse: "They took Jesus, and carrying the cross himself he went out to what is called the Place of the Skull" (John 19:16–17). I felt that God and others had given me a heavy, undeserved cross and that I was obliged to carry the burden of life on my own, without assistance, before an invisible crowd that mocked me at every step. During a six-year relapse after fourteen years of dry-drunkenness (getting rid of the "alcohol" but not dealing with the "ism"), every morning I would cry out to God, the Blessed Mother, and "the crowd" in my head for relief from the obsession to drink. If I could just "not drink," I thought, I would be okay and God would love me again. If I could manage this cross myself, then I wouldn't have to live a double life of "functioning" externally while dying internally, much like a "whitewashed tomb" (see Matthew 23:27–28). I despised the cross as well as myself.

Paraphrasing Step 1 in *Twelve Steps and Twelve Traditions*, I did not want to concede, much less accept complete defeat. It was humiliating to admit I had "warped" my mind into an obsession for self-destruction. Indeed, an act of providence helped me realize that the burdens of life and my attempts to "fix" myself were crosses of my own making. The healing miracle of the true cross of Jesus Christ transformed my sick mind, allowing me to believe his promise that if I learn from his humble and gentle heart, I will find rest for my soul. Admitting and accepting my powerlessness was the beginning of my healing journey. Jesus invited me to unite the cross of my sufferings with his own sufferings in a new way of life. Relying on the Lord and Blessed Mother in recovery has given me the grace to reflect on carrying my cross with Jesus in such a way that I can begin to see it as he did, not as an instrument of torture and humiliation but as St. Francis of Assisi expressed in his *Way of the Cross*: "When our divine Saviour beheld the cross, he most willingly stretched out his bleeding arms, lovingly embraced it, and tenderly kissed it, and placing it on his bruised shoulders, he, although almost exhausted, joyfully carried it."

Our Lord considered the Cross a gift from his Father since it was the means through which he would save us—a gift from a Father who only knows how to give his children good gifts. In this way, I have learned to carry my crosses in union with Jesus, trusting that our loving Father will draw good from them if I allow him. Yet, we can only find the strength to carry the crosses in our lives through honesty, openness, and a willingness to regularly invite the Lord to come into the Golgotha of our hearts and plant within that interior Place of the Skull a tree of new life. May God grant us the grace to carry all of our daily crosses united with Christ on our journey of recovery and healing from addictions, compulsions, and unhealthy attachments.

Pray in silence for a few moments.

Make It Personal
Share in your group or reflect in silence or by journaling if praying alone.

- Do you consider carrying your crosses as burdens to be despised and ashamed of or as opportunities for grace to be lovingly and patiently embraced?

- Where has carrying your crosses led you, and where do they continue to lead you with respect to your recovery and faith journey?

- Are you willing to ask the Holy Spirit to reveal to you how your crosses are a gift and to receive the grace of responding to them with gratitude?

The Fifth Sorrowful Mystery

THE CRUCIFIXION

Hear the Word of God
In a group setting, one person reads aloud. For individual use, read silently:

> Standing by the cross of Jesus were his mother and his mother's sister, Mary the wife of Clopas, and Mary of Magdala. When Jesus saw his mother and the disciple there whom he loved, he said to his mother, "Woman, behold your son." Then he said to the disciple, "Behold your mother." And from that hour the disciple took her into his home. After this, aware that everything was now finished, in order that the scripture might be fulfilled, Jesus said, "I thirst." There was a vessel filled with common wine. So they put a sponge soaked in wine on a sprig of hyssop and put it up to his mouth. When Jesus had taken the wine, he said, "It is finished." And bowing his head, he handed over the spirit. (John 19:25–30)

Share aloud in a group or read in silent reflection when praying alone.

- What words or images stand out to you in this reading?

- What feelings do these stir in you, or what do they cause you to think about?

- How do you want to respond to this mystery of the Crucifixion?

Pray a Decade of the Rosary
(see page xiii for instructions if needed)

A Meditation from Patty F.

This mystery reminds me of being a youngster and gazing upon Jesus crucified on the Cross, which gave me a strong sense of awe and thanksgiving. How blessed I felt that our Lord would willingly shed his blood for my sins so that I would be forgiven and the doors to heaven would be opened to me. Fifty years later, that youngster, now an adult mother, would be in the throes of the family disease of addiction. Our son Dan struggled with multiple addictions, causing much pain and suffering for us all. I felt helpless, much like Mother Mary at the foot of the Cross. One thing led to another, and the dreaded day came when we received a call from the police. Our son had died from an accidental overdose.

By the grace of God, I thought to ask the officer to please put the phone to Dan's ear so we could pray for and with him. We prayed an Our Father, a Hail Mary, and a Glory Be. We also reminded him that we loved him, God's love and mercy were there waiting for him, and we would meet again. We reminded ourselves that Mother Mary was present at Dan's death to catch him in her loving arms, just like she took her own son into her arms after his crucifixion and death.

Through the painful process of planning Dan's funeral, I kept my eyes focused on the Cross, which became crucial in helping me put one foot in front of the other. St. Paul's words from our Lord, "My grace is sufficient" (2 Corinthians 12:9), resounded often in my mind. We spent many hours at the funeral home with Dan's lifeless body, praying, sharing memories, and crying. This all gave me just a small glimpse of what Mother Mary must have gone through during her son's crucifixion. Knowing she understood my pain helped me so much. She had to trust the Father's will, just as I, too, had to trust his will in allowing my son's death. It was painfully clear that Dan was God's boy first, mine second. God became Dan's only hope, as he is for all of us! At times, Dan's death seems hard to understand, but I find solace when I keep my eyes on the Cross of Christ. On the day of Dan's funeral, when it was time to close the casket, I kissed Dan on the forehead, tucked in the little white satin lining (much like I had tucked him in so many times as my little boy), and with my family, closed the casket.

For us, it was a profound moment of "letting go and letting God." As this mystery reminds us, when we keep our eyes on the Cross, no matter our suffering and pain, God stays right there with us. By recalling that Christ suffered and died so we could be healed and forgiven, we get to know his peace and joy, even amidst the trials and storms of life. We are called to trust in his will and plan for us and our loved ones. And as we continue to gaze at the Cross with awe and thanksgiving, we come to know and accept that God's love and mercy endures forever.

Pray in silence for a few moments.

Make It Personal
Share in your group or reflect in silence or by journaling if praying alone.

- What comes to mind as you gaze upon the Cross of Christ?

- What does "let go and let God" mean to you, especially in light of difficult times?

- What role has Mother Mary played in helping you accept the Father's holy will?

THE GLORIOUS MYSTERIES

The First Glorious Mystery

THE RESURRECTION

Hear the Word of God
In a group setting, one person reads aloud. For individual use, read silently:

> But at daybreak on the first day of the week, they took the spices they had prepared and went to the tomb. They found the stone rolled away from the tomb; but when they entered, they did not find the body of the Lord Jesus. While they were puzzling over this, behold, two men in dazzling garments appeared to them. They were terrified and bowed their faces to the ground. They said to them, "Why do you seek the living one among the dead? He is not here, but he has been raised. Remember what he said to you while he was still in Galilee, that the Son of Man must be handed over to sinners and be crucified, and rise on the third day." (Luke 24:1–7)

Share aloud in a group or read in silent reflection when praying alone.

- What words or images stand out to you in this reading?

- What feelings do these stir in you, or what do they cause you to think about?

- How do you want to respond to this mystery of the Resurrection?

Pray a Decade of the Rosary
(see page xiii for instructions if needed)

A Meditation from Karen B.

The mystery of the Resurrection is relatable to almost every recovering person. It certainly is with respect to my own experience of finding recovery from the depths of addiction. The first significant event following my first few meetings of Alcoholics Anonymous was a trip to a psychiatric facility because my psychotherapist disagreed that I was an alcoholic and thought I was delusional. I was carted off to a nearby facility following her brief assessment. I tried to trust and believe her, but upon my arrival another possibility dawned on me. Maybe those AA members were right, and I should trust them more. Maybe God was indeed 100 percent in charge of 100 percent of my life's circumstances and events. Seeking God, I went into the filthy restroom of the emergency room in the psychiatric facility and got on my knees. I told God that medication, the Office of Mental Health, and my therapist could not be my Higher Power anymore. I needed proof, though. I was an abject nonbeliever. But not for long.

I got up, washed my hands, and opened the door to see a local AA member fondly known as "Stuttering Walt" standing before me. My proof had arrived quickly, and it was a baptismal moment for me. Jesus experienced a foretaste of his passion, death, and resurrection while submerged in the baptismal waters of the Jordan. In a similar way, this spiritual experience in the emergency room offered me hope for an ongoing resurrection experience. My life changed forever in that instant. I had encountered the beginning of a resurrected life.

Many of us have touched the floor of hell only to be raised up to kiss the face of God through the gifts of 12-step recovery. We are grateful for our personal powerlessness because it brought us to our knees and gave us the gift of willingness—the key to lasting change and an ongoing, daily resurrection of mind, body, and spirit as well as freedom from the slavery of addictions, compulsions, and unhealthy attachments. This mystery reminds us that the risen Christ is alive in us and occupies the entire universe, always giving us his forgiveness and salvific love as long as we seek him with faith and hope.

The Glorious Mysteries 81

Pray in silence for a few moments.

Make It Personal
Share in your group or reflect in silence or by journaling if praying alone.

- Do you consider your recovery a true resurrection—a deliverance from a life of sin—and, if so, what are your daily reminders of this?

- What emotions did you experience when you emerged from the dark world of shame, fear, and regret of active addiction and into the light of resurrection and Christ's unconditional love for you?

- In what ways are you living as a new creation, resurrected in, with, and through our Lord and his passion?

The Second Glorious Mystery

THE ASCENSION OF THE LORD

Hear the Word of God
In a group setting, one person reads aloud. For individual use, read silently:

> Then he led them [out] as far as Bethany, raised his hands, and blessed them. As he blessed them he parted from them and was taken up to heaven. They did him homage and then returned to Jerusalem with great joy, and they were continually in the temple praising God. (Luke 24:50–53)

Share aloud in a group or read in silent reflection when praying alone.

- What words or images stand out to you in this reading?

- What feelings do these stir in you, or what do they cause you to think about?

- How do you want to respond to this mystery of the Ascension of the Lord?

Pray a Decade of the Rosary
(see page xiii for instructions if needed)

A Meditation from Bill B.

I imagine the scene depicted in this mystery as one under a bright blue sky and accompanied by a gentle breeze, the apostles gathered on the hillside. The men are silent, looking to Mary for strength. For a long time, I imagined this mystery as one of sorrow and loss. Jesus is leaving everyone behind. His mother would be alone now without a husband or son. The apostles are in grief, looking up to heaven as Jesus fades from view. Yet, the gospel tells us they had "great joy." I then imagined that Jesus, too, must have felt joy because he was escaping the cruel and evil world and returning to the Father. But this was only a projection of my own addictive thought patterns and tendency to seek escape from pain. Jesus does not ascend to escape from this world. He ascends so he can be more present and accessible to us through his Spirit and sacraments. Just as Jesus ascended to reclaim his throne, we too are called to rise up and claim our vocation as his beloved sons and daughters. And just as Mary and the apostles had to be willing to give up the bodily presence of the Lord to embrace the Spirit, we too must be willing to let go of our old life of addiction to embrace a new life of grace.

My experience in active addiction began with a desire to escape the pain of past trauma and ended in ever-deeper guilt and isolation. Lying in bed one night after a particularly desperate relapse, I listened to the hollow sound of my heart pounding in the dark silence. I had found myself in this condition a hundred times before. I raced through my usual mental exercises, seeking to justify and distance myself from what I had done. However, this time was different. No matter how hard I tried, I couldn't find an escape. I was no longer able to conjure excuses to absolve myself. I knew there was nobody other than myself to blame for my addictive behavior. With my conscience in anguish, I realized that I had lost the grace of God and couldn't face him. I didn't have anyone else to turn to either. Years of engaging in my compulsive addiction had driven others away from me. I was out to sea, and the waters of despair were pulling me down.

Then, in the midst of that guilt-stricken turbulence, I noticed something on the nightstand I had completely forgotten. In a tangled clump under the lamp was a welcome sight: the beads of the Rosary I had turned to in times past. I knew then the Rosary was my lifeline—a connection to someone who would listen. In that dark hour, Mother Mary became my only hope. She was the hand that could pull me out of the surging waters. She was my refuge for sinners.

While my thoughts of God envisioned only his justified wrath blazing against me for a multitude of sins, the Blessed

The Glorious Mysteries 85

Mother seemed to look upon me with sorrow and compassion. As the Rosary beads passed through my fingers and I prayed the mysteries, a certain light came to my mind. I finally accepted that I needed help. I couldn't fight this battle alone. As my prayers reached the mystery of the Ascension, one word emerged: victory. Jesus had taken his throne in triumph, and God would win a similar victory for me. I only needed to surrender in faith, take action, and get the support of others. That was my first step toward finding sobriety through Catholic in Recovery. That allowed for my own ascension toward healing.

This mystery is a reminder that Jesus is always with us. Through the Church—the true temple of God on earth—Jesus remains present to us through prayer, Mass, Eucharistic Adoration, and Confession. We can also encounter him regularly through Catholic in Recovery, where I have learned to finally share my struggles with a community of believers who understand them because they have gone through the same things themselves. By trusting God and seeking the fellowship of others, we too can ascend with Christ from the depths of addiction, compulsions, and unhealthy attachments to the heights of sobriety and freedom.

Pray in silence for a few moments.

Make It Personal
Share in your group or reflect in silence or by journaling if praying alone.

- Why do you think the apostles felt joy at the Ascension even though Jesus "parted from them"?

- What would it mean for you to rise above the concerns and fears that weigh you down?

- How important is a community of believers in your ongoing recovery?

The Third Glorious Mystery

THE COMING OF THE HOLY SPIRIT

Hear the Word of God
In a group setting, one person reads aloud. For individual use, read silently:

> When the time for Pentecost was fulfilled, they were all in one place together. And suddenly there came from the sky a noise like a strong driving wind, and it filled the entire house in which they were. Then there appeared to them tongues as of fire, which parted and came to rest on each one of them. And they were all filled with the holy Spirit and began to speak in different tongues, as the Spirit enabled them to proclaim. (Acts 2:1–4)

Share aloud in a group or read in silent reflection when praying alone.

- What words or images stand out to you in this reading?

- What feelings do these stir in you, or what do they cause you to think about?

- How do you want to respond to this mystery of the Coming of the Holy Spirit?

Pray a Decade of the Rosary
(see page xiii for instructions if needed)

A Meditation from Paola P.

As I consider this mystery, it brings me great joy to reflect on the powerful experience of encountering the Holy Spirit in my own life and what it meant for him to overshadow me. My spiritual journey through the Twelve Steps of recovery has profoundly transformed my relationship with God, revealing different facets of his character during various seasons of my life. We have a saying in the program that we don't work the Steps, they work us. They are meant to be experienced. I'm reminded of a time during my Step work when I was seeking and drawing closer to the Holy Spirit.

My alcoholic husband had not yet found recovery and was progressively getting worse. He had lost his job, friends, and prestige. I sensed that something had to "break." It felt like I needed to make a decision after working my program for a few

The Glorious Mysteries 89

years. I was desperate to leave my marriage, but I did not have the "release" from God. I was praying for God's will for my life.

I was in a season of "minding my own business," literally. I had taken up a woodworking and DIY hobby for building Jesse Trees (wooden artworks representing Jesus's family tree) and was trying to sell them all over town. My heart was heavy, but my car was filled with worship music. I came across a billboard sign on the highway that had one word: ADVENT. It caught my attention because it seemed a peculiar word for a secular advertisement. As I drove closer, I realized the trees were covering the full word: ADVENTURE. I had then what recovery fellowship calls "a moment of clarity." I had never seen that word within another word (I'm more of a math person), and I felt the Spirit of God say to my spirit that I was going to go on an adventure that upcoming Advent. Another thought rolled into my head: *I wonder if there is a book out there called the Advent Adventure?*

Sure enough, the first book I pulled up online was a Jesse Tree devotional with that same title! I felt convicted that I had heard the voice of God and his will for my life. I knew I was on the right track and exactly where I was supposed to be—I felt confident trusting that he was with me. This led me to a church that was Spirit-filled. I asked my husband if he would like to attend with me, knowing he would probably say no, but he said yes. The church was three hours away, but I wanted to know what revival felt like. I wanted to know what the woman hemorrhaging felt when she touched the garment of Jesus. I wanted to encounter the Spirit of the living God!

We attended a healing service, and the man of God at the pulpit asked my husband and me to approach. He laid his hands over us to pray, and he began to prophesy over our lives. I felt a physical power come upon me that knocked me down to the floor with great strength. I had no choice but to fall! Both my husband and I had never experienced the presence of God's Spirit in that way, and the words that were spoken over us are still coming to pass. My husband found recovery from his alcoholism shortly after that. I began to see the changes in him as he found a sponsor that very Advent season. Praise God, for his mercy endures forever!

Since then, now a few years ago, I can say that my life has never again been the same after being touched like that by the Holy Spirit—touched very much, I imagine, like the apostles during Pentecost. My prayers are more fruitful. My ability to discern God's will has grown. I have come to love the voice of God and to realize we are called to live the Christian life, work our recovery, and participate in the sacraments from a place of victory—even in the midst of our sufferings. Our identities come from God, and it is he who specializes in helping the hopeless, especially those struggling with addictions, compulsions, and unhealthy attachments, as well as their loved ones. We are simply called to see him and allow his Spirit to be present in our lives. In other words, we are called to do what Step 11 encourages us to do—improve our ability to carry the presence of God throughout our days. And this is a joyful adventure like no other.

Pray in silence for a few moments.

Make It Personal
Share in your group or reflect in silence or by journaling if praying alone.

- How might the experience of being "overshadowed" by the Holy Spirit reveal deeper truths about your identity in God and purpose in life?

- How can the act of seeking and improving your conscious contact with God through prayer and meditation open you up to the Holy Spirit's influence in your daily life?

- In what ways have you experienced the presence of the Holy Spirit in your life, and how did it transform your understanding of God's love and guidance?

The Fourth Glorious Mystery

THE ASSUMPTION OF MARY

Hear the Word of God
In a group setting, one person reads aloud. For individual use, read silently:

> The Immaculate Mother of God, the ever-Virgin Mary, having completed the course of her earthly life, was assumed body and soul into heavenly glory. (Pope Pius XII, *Munificentissimus Deus*)

Share aloud in a group or read in silent reflection when praying alone.

- What words or images stand out to you in this reading?

- What feelings do these stir in you, or what do they cause you to think about?

- How do you want to respond to this mystery of the Assumption of Mary?

Pray a Decade of the Rosary
(see page xiii for instructions if needed)

A Meditation from Kay P.

I imagine I'm not alone in having trouble considering the Glorious Mysteries in a sensible framework. Having no firsthand experience of seeing a resurrection or experiencing a heavenly event, I glean my understanding through scripture references and my imagination. I do recall meditating once on eternal life and thinking, *If I'm lucky, my resurrected body will be so slender and graceful!* Still, death is something I don't want to spend too much time thinking about. To this day, I can still hear the voices of my older cousins teasing me with the refrain from "The Hearse Song": "The worms crawl in, the worms crawl out...." With all this in mind, it always appealed to me to begin my Rosary reflection of this mystery with the phrase "Jesus loved his mother so much that he did not want her body to undergo corruption at death." Recalling that we are both body and soul made in the image of God, it is natural that bodily decay would repel us. We are meant to recognize our unique dignity among all of creation! But do we live this way?

In my own experience, I've been a food addict as far back as I can remember. Like for many people who struggle with unhealthy attachments, addiction is often multigenerational. I grew up in a loving home, but my dad was a functioning alcoholic. In other words, he was very successful and well regarded in the workplace during the day, but when he came home at night he would drink until he went to bed. To his credit, he never hung out in bars or taverns (like both my grandfathers did), and to my recollection, he never drove while inebriated, but his temper was easily roused and he often yelled to get his point across. As a young child, I turned to food to ease the tension of always "walking on eggshells" around him. I didn't begin drinking alcohol until college and considered myself a social drinker.

I remember going for a job interview once, and we toured a facility for individuals who had severely lost brain function due to alcoholism. I stepped into a classroom setting with all these adult individuals sitting there while the instructor recited, "Today is Tuesday. Yesterday was Monday. Tomorrow will be Wednesday." The class, many of them with blank stares, had difficulty repeating after her. I had no idea that alcohol could have such a devastating effect on the brain. I vowed to never allow alcohol to get such a grip on my life, but in my thirties, food didn't seem to sufficiently numb the tension, and I began to drink wine daily.

As one who spent many years indulging in my unhealthy attachments, I allowed both my body and my soul to experience corruption. Succumbing to my specific addictions (food and alcohol) led to almost daily incidents of misbehavior, as I snuck food and ate in secret, drank in excess, and lived in denial. I allowed the substances of my addiction to biochemically alter my mood and behavior, becoming irritable, impatient, controlling, and argumentative. Obviously, beyond the wreckage to relationships my addictions caused, they beat up my body also. Through years of binge eating and yo-yo dieting, I developed a

The Glorious Mysteries 95

variety of serious health issues (many of which will remain with me for life) and to this day have extreme shame regarding my appearance. I also noted further damage alcohol can do to the body beyond impaired brain function. I'm just vain enough to realize that the drinking I was doing caused my skin color to appear bilious, my eyes to lose their vibrancy, and my wrinkles to be compounded! In short, through my own choices, I assisted my soul and body in becoming corrupt.

The good news is that God, through his mercy and grace, continued to put people and situations on my path to help me break the cycle of corruption. In working the Twelve Steps, I've been able to be *honest* about my dependency on food and alcohol; *open* to listening to those sharing their experience, strength, and hope; and *willing* to do whatever it takes to free myself from my unhealthy attachments. Now I'm better able to cope with the inconveniences and disruptions of daily life without "flying off the handle." I don't feel that I need to be the center of attention and give my unsolicited advice or, rather, oversight to others. It's amazing how relationships that I used to think were toxic are now easier—and the only thing that changed was me!

As we meditate on this mystery, let us celebrate that God is working to heal the corruption we have allowed within our bodies and souls due to our addictions, compulsions, and unhealthy attachments. That is truly a glorious truth! And although our current transformation is not one from the earthly realm to the heavenly realm, let us remember that Jesus wants to give us a gift similar to what he gave his mother—a resurrected body that freely and joyfully glorifies him forever.

Pray in silence for a few moments.

Make It Personal
Share in your group or reflect in silence or by journaling if praying alone.

- In what ways have you experienced corruption as a result of your addictions, compulsions, or unhealthy attachments (or the family spiritual disease of addiction)?

- What are some events or situations that our Lord used to get your attention about the effects of your behavior?

- Do you see transformation in your life from working the Twelve Steps, and if so, how?

The Fifth Glorious Mystery

THE CORONATION OF MARY

Hear the Word of God
In a group setting, one person reads aloud. For individual use, read silently:

> Mary, the Virgin Mother of God, reigns with a mother's solicitude over the entire world, just as she is crowned in heavenly blessedness with the glory of a Queen. (Pope Pius XII, *Ad Caeli Reginam*)

Share aloud in a group or read in silent reflection when praying alone.

- What words or images stand out to you in this reading?

- What feelings do these stir in you, or what do they cause you to think about?

- How do you want to respond to this mystery of the Coronation of Mary?

Pray a Decade of the Rosary
(see page xiii for instructions if needed)

A Meditation from Joanne R.

There are two thoughts that come to my mind as I reflect on the Coronation of Mary. The first is an acknowledgment that Mary is Queen of Heaven and Earth. The second is the fruit that emerges when we ask for Mary's powerful intercession. Both of these insights played a major part in my recovery.

My addiction started during my sophomore year of college after I lost my hometown boyfriend in a car accident. I was raised in a traditional Catholic home, but in my teen years I drifted away from my faith, and by college I was only marginally Catholic. The death of my boyfriend had me seriously doubting God's existence. My parents did not allow me to attend the wake or funeral, fearing I wouldn't return to college, and as a result, I dealt with my painful feelings by using cocaine. I did not want to deal with my negative feelings, and so began my addiction. After graduating college, I ended up in Aspen, Colorado, where my life was filled with sex, drugs, and rock and roll. I hung out with famous recording artists, such as John Denver, Jimmy Buffett, and the Eagles, and the only time I went to church was when I was in trouble or distress. However, I soon tired of this lifestyle and returned to Illinois, where I grew up.

I started working a corporate job, though I was still using cocaine. I felt unfulfilled and that something was missing in

The Glorious Mysteries 99

my life. One night I went to a Catholic parish to play bingo, and upon going into the church's basement, I heard a voice say, "You should be going upstairs." I looked upstairs and saw the tabernacle. This really shook me, and I thought I was losing my mind. I started attending Mass at this parish, and eventually I started working with a youth group at a priest's insistence, though it bothered me that I was working with youth while still using drugs. The priest had planned a trip to Medjugorje (in Bosnia and Herzegovina), and I agreed to go only if we went through Italy because I wanted a Gucci purse. Off I went with forty teenagers and twenty adults to Medjugorje, not believing that the Queen of Heaven and Earth was actually appearing there. But I had a powerful experience that would change my life forever. This experience revealed to me that I had to alter my life and get off drugs. I realized Jesus was to be the center of my life and that, as St. John the Baptist said, "He must increase; I must decrease" (John 3:30).

On returning from Medjugorje, I wanted my conversion to be effortless, with no pain or suffering. Well, it didn't happen that way. Sr. Charla, a nun who was instrumental in putting the pilgrimage together, told me that the best thing for my conversion was to consecrate my life to the Blessed Mother through St. Louis de Montfort's "Total Consecration of Jesus through Mary." I realized that as a queen, Mary not only intercedes for us but also acts as her son's mediator. As the Queen of Heaven and Earth, she is entrusted to distribute God's graces. I consecrated my life to Mary, our Queen, and so began my recovery.

Our Lady soon brought Fr. Charlie B. into my life, who introduced me to the Twelve Steps, and I joined Narcotics Anonymous. I worked the Twelve Steps, went to counseling, prayed the Rosary daily, and went to monthly Confession and Eucharistic Adoration, and all of these graces helped me stay true to my recovery program. By believing that the Queen of Heaven and Earth is a powerful intercessor for us, I grew in my faith and recovery. There is no heart purer or more in tune with Jesus than Mary's. As we meditate on this mystery, let us regularly call out to our great intercessor, Mary, Queen of Heaven and Earth, and ask her for her help in growing closer to her son in our recovery and faith. And let us turn to Mary with tender trust, one day at a time.

Pray in silence for a few moments.

Make It Personal
Share in your group or reflect in silence or by journaling if praying alone.

- What role has Mary, Queen of Heaven and Earth, played in your own recovery?

- How can you make it more of a habit to ask the saints, especially Mary, to intercede for you and your loved ones?

- Have you considered consecrating yourself to the Blessed Mother? What has been the outcome?

ADDITIONAL PRAYERS

The Memorare, which means "remember" in Latin, is a Marian prayer that became popular in the seventeenth century. The prayer serves as an invocation of the Blessed Mother to intercede for us on behalf of her son, Jesus.

Memorare

> Remember, O most gracious Virgin Mary,
> that never was it known that anyone who fled to thy protection,
> implored thy help, or sought thy intercession,
> was left unaided.
> Inspired by this confidence,
> I fly unto thee, O Virgin of virgins, my Mother.
> To thee do I come, before thee I stand, sinful and sorrowful.
> O Mother of the Word Incarnate,
> despise not my petitions,
> but in your mercy, hear and answer me.
> Amen.

The Angelus commemorates the angel Gabriel's annunciation to Mary as well as the Resurrection of the Lord. Traditionally, it was said three times a day (morning, noon, and evening), though it can be said anytime as an invitation for the Blessed Mother's intercession.

The Angelus

V. The Angel of the Lord declared to Mary.
R. And she conceived of the Holy Spirit.
V. Hail Mary, full of grace, the Lord is with thee;
Blessed art thou among women
and blessed is the fruit of thy womb, Jesus.
R. Holy Mary, Mother of God,
pray for us sinners, now
and at the hour of our death. Amen.
V. Behold the handmaid of the Lord.
R. Be it done unto me according to Thy word.
V. Hail Mary, full of grace, the Lord is with thee;
Blessed art thou among women
and blessed is the fruit of thy womb, Jesus.
R. Holy Mary, Mother of God,
pray for us sinners, now
and at the hour of our death. Amen.
V. And the Word was made flesh.
R. And dwelt among us.
V. Hail Mary, full of grace, the Lord is with thee;
Blessed art thou among women
and blessed is the fruit of thy womb, Jesus.
R. Holy Mary, Mother of God,
pray for us sinners, now
and at the hour of our death. Amen.
V. Pray for us, O Holy Mother of God,

R. that we may be made worthy of the promises of Christ.
V. Let us pray:
Pour forth, we beseech thee, O Lord,
thy grace into our hearts;
that we, to whom the incarnation of Christ, thy Son,
was made known by the message of an angel,
may by his Passion and Cross be brought to
the glory of his Resurrection,
through the same Christ, Our Lord.
R. Amen.

The Magnificat is a prayer recited by the Blessed Mother when pregnant with Jesus in Luke's gospel. It is Mary's song of praise to the Lord, and one that we can pray along with her in adoration of God.

The Magnificat

My soul proclaims the greatness of the Lord,
my spirit rejoices in God my Savior,
for he has looked with favor on his humble servant.
From this day all generations will call me blessed;
the Almighty has done great things for me,
and holy is his Name.
He has mercy on those who fear Him
in every generation.
He has shown the strength of his arm,

he has scattered the proud in their conceit.
He has cast down the mighty from their thrones,
and has lifted up the humble.
He has filled the hungry with good things,
and the rich he has sent away empty.
He has come to the help of his servant Israel
for he has remembered his promise of mercy,
the promise he made to our fathers,
to Abraham and his children forever.
Glory to the Father, and to the Son, and to the Holy
    Spirit,
as it was in the beginning, is now, and will be forever.
Amen, Alleluia.

The Serenity Prayer, attributed to theologian Reinhold Niebuhr in the 1940s and widely embraced in 12-step recovery programs, serves as a guiding mantra for individuals seeking peace and strength in their journey toward sobriety and personal growth. The full prayer aligns with a Catholic understanding of Jesus Christ as our Savior and Higher Power and encourages surrender, acceptance, and trust.

Serenity Prayer

God,
Grant me the serenity
to accept the things I cannot change

the courage to change the things I can
and the wisdom to know the difference.
Living one day at a time,
enjoying one moment at a time,
accepting hardship as the pathway to peace.
Taking, as he did, this sinful world as it is,
not as I would have it.
Trusting that he will make all things right
if I surrender to his will.
That I may be reasonably happy in this life
and supremely happy with him forever in the next.
Amen.

The St. Francis Prayer, attributed to St. Francis of Assisi, emphasizes peace, love, and selflessness, encouraging individuals to be instruments of harmony and healing in the world. In 12-step recovery programs, it is often referred to as the "Eleventh Step Prayer" and serves as a powerful reminder to cultivate compassion, humility, and service to others.

St. Francis Prayer

Lord,
Make me an instrument of your peace.
Where there is hatred, let me bring love.
Where there is injury, pardon.
Where there is doubt, faith.

Where there is despair, hope.
Where there is darkness, light.
Where there is sadness, joy.
Where there is discord, harmony.
Where there is error, truth.
Where there is wrong, the spirit of forgiveness.
O Divine Master,
Grant that I may not so much seek
to be consoled as to console,
to be understood as to understand,
to be loved as to love.
For it is in giving that we receive,
it is in pardoning that we are pardoned,
and it is in dying that we are born to eternal life.
Amen.

The Third Step Prayer, often used in 12-step recovery programs, expresses a commitment to surrender one's will to God, seeking guidance and strength to live a life aligned with spiritual principles and sharing the Gospel as a testament to Christ's healing.

The Third Step Prayer

God,
I offer myself to thee
to build with me and to do with me as thou wilt.

Relieve me of the bondage of self, that I may better do thy will.
Take away my difficulties, that victory over them may bear witness
to those I would help of thy Power, thy Love, and thy Way of life.
May I do thy will always!
Amen.

The Seventh Step Prayer, a key element in 12-step recovery, reflects a humble request for help in overcoming shortcomings and emphasizes the willingness to let go of defects of character in order to grow spiritually and serve others.

The Seventh Step Prayer

My Creator,
I am now willing that you should have all of me,
the good and the bad.
I pray that you now remove from me
every single defect of character
which stands in the way of my usefulness
to you and my fellows.
Grant me strength, as I go out from here,
to do your bidding.
Amen.

Scott Weeman is the founder of Catholic in Recovery, a community of individuals and families seeking freedom from various addictions, compulsions, and unhealthy attachments. He is the author of *The Twelve Steps and the Sacraments* and *The Catholic in Recovery Workbook*. Weeman's Catholic in Recovery organization won the top prize in the OSV Institute for Catholic Innovation Challenge Showcase in 2021.

Weeman holds a master's degree in clinical counseling from Point Loma Nazarene University and serves as a marriage and family therapist in addition to his ministry work. He has appeared on EWTN's *The Journey Home*, *Women of Grace*, and *EWTN Live* and is a recurring guest on *Catholic Answers Live*. His work has been featured on Hallow, Aleteia, and Patheos.

He lives in Nashville, Tennessee, with his wife and three children.

catholicinrecovery.com
Instagram: @scottweeman
Facebook: @scottweeman51
X: Scott_Weeman

Catholic in Recovery (CIR) is a community of men and women around the world that provides hope and healing to individuals and families impacted by addictions, compulsions, and unhealthy attachments by integrating 12-step recovery principles with the sacraments and traditions of the Catholic Church. CIR accomplishes its mission by offering in-person and virtual 12-step meetings, retreats, and resources blending 12-step wisdom with the Catholic faith. Catholic in Recovery won the top prize in the OSV Institute for Catholic Innovation Challenge Showcase in 2021.

catholicinrecovery.com
Instagram: @catholicinrecovery
Facebook: @catholicinrecovery
YouTube: Catholic in Recovery

MORE RESOURCES
for Catholics in Recovery and Those Moving Toward It

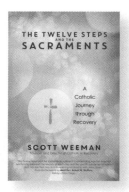

In the first book to directly integrate the Twelve Steps with the practice of Catholicism, Scott Weeman, founder and director of Catholic in Recovery, pairs his personal story with compassionate straight talk to show Catholics how to bridge the commonly felt gap between the Higher Power of 12-step programs and the merciful God that he rediscovered in the heart of the sacraments.

The Catholic in Recovery Workbook is the first step-by-step guide for working through the Twelve Steps of recovery from a Catholic perspective. If you struggle with addiction, compulsions, or unhealthy attachments—or love someone who does—this book will help you to discover the life-changing mercy of Jesus Christ through Church tradition and the grace of the sacraments.

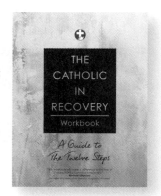

Find these titles wherever books and eBooks are sold.
Learn more at **avemariapress.com**.